This book about

Jesus and the Storm

belongs to

Jesus was very busy.
There always seemed to
be a lot of people wanting
to see him.

One evening, he said to his close
friends, "Come, let's go in our boat
across to the other side of the lake."

His friends got into the boat with him.

In the boat, Jesus soon fell
asleep.

Suddenly a strong wind began
to blow.

The waves began to crash
against the sides of the boat.

The waves began to
spill into the boat.

"Wake up and help us,"
shouted Jesus' friends.
"We are going to sink
with the boat!"

Jesus stood up.

"Be quiet," he said to the waves.
"Be still," he said to the wind.

Then everything was calm.
Everything that was dark and
dangerous and scary just went away.

The day came, bright and clear.

"What made you so scared?" asked
Jesus. "Don't you believe in God?"

Jesus' friends knew they were safe,
but they were more scared than ever.

"Who is our friend Jesus?" they
asked each other. "Who can he be?
Even the wind and waves obey him."

Special Words

lake a pond as big as a sea

obey to do as you are asked

quiet when waves are quiet, they lie down

sink a boat that sinks goes down, down, down

still when the wind is still, it stops blowing

A Prayer

Dear God, look from your heaven
Upon my boat and me;
Protect me from the billows
Of the great and stormy sea.

Published by Lion Children's Books
an imprint of
Lion Hudson plc
Wilkinson House, Jordan Hill Road,
Oxford OX2 8DR, England
www.lionhudson.com/lionchildrens
ISBN 978 0 7459 6311 2
e-ISBN 978 0 7459 6745 5

First edition 2011

A catalogue record for this book is available from the British Library

Printed and bound in China, January 2015, LH06